# "Man—with Variations"

# "Man—with Variations"
## Interviews with Franz Boas and Colleagues, 1937

Joseph Mitchell

Edited and with an introduction
by Robert Brightman

PRICKLY PARADIGM PRESS
CHICAGO

Main text ©2017 by the Estate of Joseph Mitchell.
Introduction ©2017 by Robert Brightman.

Prickly Paradigm Press, LLC
5629 South University Avenue
Chicago, IL 60637

www.prickly-paradigm.com

ISBN: 9780996635516
LCCN: 2016960853

Printed in the United States of America on acid-free paper.

# Introduction

Joseph Mitchell is the chronicler of an earlier New York City's odder citizens, a pre-inventor of New Journalism, and, in Calvin Trillin's words, "the *New Yorker* writer who set the standard." He is plausibly America's finest literary journalist. Mitchell began his career as a reporter for the *New York Herald Tribune* and the *New York World-Telegram* in the 1930s. In 1938, the year he joined *The New Yorker*, Mitchell published *My Ears Are Bent*, a collection of his newspaper writing. In the foreword, he candidly described his most and least favored interview subjects.

> The only people I do not care to listen to are society women, industrial leaders, distinguished authors, ministers, explorers, moving picture actors (except W. C. Fields and Stepin Fetchit), and any actress under the age of thirty-five. I believe the most interesting human beings, so far

as talk is concerned, are anthropologists, farmers, prostitutes, psychiatrists, and the occasional bartender.

Anthropologists? Their inclusion here in the exalted company of farmers, prostitutes, and bartenders is over-determined—but points most directly to an assignment Mitchell completed the preceding year.

## The Interviews

Sometime during 1937, while working for the *World-Telegram*, Mitchell was contacted by Jack Sargent Harris, his friend and shipmate on a 1931 freighter excursion to Leningrad. Harris was now a doctoral candidate in Columbia University's Department of Anthropology. An obituary by Kevin Yelvington notes that Harris studied with Ruth Benedict, Ralph Linton, and Alexander Lesser, and worked also as Franz Boas' assistant in his ongoing research on immigrant gesture.

On Mitchell's initiative, Harris arranged a meeting with Boas, and Boas then agreed to a Mitchell-authored *World-Telegram* article on anthropology with himself and his Columbia colleagues as subjects. There was seemingly some editorial resistance at the paper. Mitchell observed in the foreword to *My Ears Are Bent* that "it is not easy to get an interview with Professor Franz Boas, the greatest anthropologist in the world, across a city desk." The project was, however, approved, and a six-part series based on interviews with Boas and others in the Columbia anthropology orbit appeared from November 1 to November 6, 1937. Reprinted now for the first time, they comprise the body of this Prickly Paradigm pamphlet.

What is known of the Mitchell-Boas encounter —and what the two men made of it—derives exclusively from Mitchell's recollections related over fifty years later to Thomas Kunkel: these are briefly described in Kunkel's 2015 biography of Mitchell. Since Kunkel began this latter book after Mitchell's death in 1996, the topic of anthropology seemingly arose during prior interviews with Mitchell for Kunkel's biography of *New Yorker* editor Harold Ross. Anthropology is not mentioned in other Mitchell interviews published or summarized by Norman Sims and Ben Yagoda. Additional relevant material may exist in the Joseph Mitchell Papers in the New York Public Library.

As Kunkel recounts, Mitchell remembered the interview dynamics with Boas as unexpectedly symmetrical:

> As the two men settled into conversation, the reporter began to realize that Boas was paying more attention to him than to his questions, essentially an anthropologist observing a curious specimen—the New York newspaperman. Boas was becoming increasingly engaged—"not in me," Mitchell explained, "but in my ignorance." As Boas tried to explain his research principles, he suddenly told Mitchell, "Read this," and handed him a copy of his book *Anthropology and Modern Life*, which Mitchell would in fact read, and he "began telling me how to look at the world. He said, 'Don't take anything for granted, don't take yourself for granted, or your father.'" Mitchell was exhilarated by it all. He would remember coming away from the experience "feeling born again."

In the *World-Telegram* series, Mitchell described Boas' book as one "which can be read with a minimum of pain by laymen."

## The *World-Telegram* Series

It remains an interesting but unfathomable question how the priorities of Boas and other interview subjects, Mitchell's editors, and Mitchell himself interacted to shape the anthropology series. People familiar with Mitchell's writing will discover in it both traces of earlier newspaper work and intimations of what was to come at *The New Yorker*.

Titled "Man—with Variations," the series contains six separately named installments. Each installment, in turn, divides into sections with eye-catching headings, as with "Succeeded by Woman" for the section describing Ruth Benedict's interim position as acting chair. The first piece featured an imposing drawing of Boas, and each was accompanied by photographs.

Although Mitchell had some conception of the scope of Boasian anthropology—"linguistics, primitive mentality, folklore, ethnology, growth and senility, the physical effects of environment"—he may have despaired of rationalizing its unity, for the series profiles the cultural and physical subfields. The series is divisible into two parts, the first comprising two installments focusing on Boas and "race." "Anthropologists Smile as Hitler Talks of His 'Pure Germany'" introduces both Boas and the field of anthropology. "Anthropology," wrote Mitchell, "is the study of man as he lives in social groups, and it embraces a whole array of sciences." "Enormously Learned Dr. Boas,

Outstanding Anthropologist, at 78 Is Most Dangerous Foe of Hitler's Racial Concepts" contains an extended biographical treatment of Boas. Respect and personal liking are evident in Mitchell's descriptions of Boas' versatility, international reputation, disciplinary eminence, and formative role as teacher.

Both pieces emphasize the topicality of Boas' critique of racial formalisms and determinisms relative to the Nuremburg Race Laws enacted in Germany two years earlier. There is, predictably, no explicit mention of Jim Crow laws or disenfranchisement in the United States. But in language crafted to unsettle some *World-Telegram* readers' taken-for-granted assumptions, Mitchell put across Boas' findings:

> Dr. Boas knows that the term "race" is vague and approximate, and that there is no such thing as a "pure race," and he doubts if there is any "superior race."

These remarks were elaborated with lengthy quotes by Boas and excerpts from a written summary by Benedict, passages which some readers might have found hard going. Mitchell, never averse to irony, reported that the University of Kiel, having earlier awarded Boas an honorary M.D., had recently ceremonially incinerated his books; photographs of this event accompany the article. Mitchell also noted Boas' reaction: "If people want to be crazy, what can you do about it?"

The second part of the series comprises four installments describing research by Boas' students and colleagues. "Average Anthropologist Gets a $500 Grant to Do a Miracle—and He Generally Does, Groping for Ghost of the Past" reports Ruth Landes'

Ojibwe ethnography and linguist Edward Kennard's Mandan fieldwork experiences. "Primitive Music of Aborigines is Preserved for Posterity" is devoted to George Herzog's studies of African and Native North American music. "Aged Pawnee Recalls Laws and Rituals of Ancestors" covers Gene Weltfish and Alexander Lesser's Pawnee research. "People of Dobu Behave a Lot Like People on the Subway" describes Reo Fortune's Dobuan research and fieldwork as mediated by his friend and Columbia mentor Benedict. Mitchell describes Benedict as the Department's "acting executive officer" after Boas' retirement earlier in 1937. Ralph Linton is conspicuously absent from the article. Possibly Linton had yet to arrive on-site as departmental chairman. Yelvington says that Harris, Mitchell's friend and conduit to Boas, "adored" Benedict and "deplored" Linton.

These four pieces show Mitchell's interests in relativism, fieldwork, and the uses of speech and memory. Mitchell appreciated the Boasian critique of provincially Western conventions generalized as human universals:

> Many of the laws and principles of [Western social] sciences are based entirely on data drawn from our own, or Western, civilization, and ... many of them, as a matter of fact, break down when checked against the discoveries of anthropologists.

So, for example, with acquisitive "instincts." Mitchell also described commensurabilities of primitive with civilized cultural forms, quoting Herzog's observation that indigenous and Western musics alike have histories and formal properties. Melancholy nostalgia for the vanishing primitive infuses the articles. Assuming a future in which civilization will "warp" indigenous societies, Mitchell emphasized the priority Boas gave to documentation and reconstruction. Thus, for example, Lesser's work with the last speaker of the Caddoan language Kitsai or Herzog's wax cylinders that "will be here when the Indians are long gone."

Salvage agendas notwithstanding, Mitchell described Boas' research on gesture in contemporary New York immigrant populations. He was also conversant with nascent acculturation research on the "reservation Indian who, perhaps, eats corn flakes for breakfast and believes firmly in the Townsend plan." Juxtapositions of indigenous culture with contemporary interests and participations interested Mitchell. He described consultant Mark Evarts, walking encyclopedia of Pawnee custom, as

> a baseball and prize fight fan. He listens to sports on the radio. He says he predicted the defeat of Joe Louis. He said, however, that he didn't bet against him. "If I have money," he once explained, "I don't bet on fights. I buy beer."

Slightly over a decade later, Mitchell wrote "The Mohawks in High Steel" about Kahnawake Mohawks in the construction industry. The article remarks on younger Kahnawakes' antipathy to Pan-Indian images and stereotypes.

Mitchell was at pains to put across that anthropology is more than "collecting weird facts," but he was not averse to uses of believe-it-or-not exotica. Thus his account of Ruth Landes' Ojibwe research begins with women warriors and shamans, before proceeding to windigos and cannibals. Here Mitchell's reporting preserves infelicitous qualities of the then-ascendant culture and personality orientation: "Until about twelve years ago the Ojibwa were murderously paranoiac." Speaking of paranoia, Mitchell's sketch of Fortune's Dobuan research came primarily, perhaps exclusively, through Benedict. Mitchell identified her as a source but omitted that many passages were taken verbatim from *Patterns of Culture*. Not unexpectedly, the Dobu coverage foregrounds treachery, competition, sorcery, cannibalism, devalued laughter, predatory in-laws, and onerous bride-service. But Mitchell went beyond Benedict by finding in Dobu tropes that could evoke shocked recognition and unexpected familiarity among the New York natives. Homeward-bound on the subway, strap-hanging, *World-Telegram* readers could learn of the savage Dobuans' likeness to themselves:

> The thief is exalted if he can get away with it, people engage in endless business deals simply for the pleasure involved, cut-throat competition is the basis of all endeavor, and the people are always as dour and set-faced as the people in a subway.

Mitchell did not ignore less spectacular ethnographic topics. His careful description of Pawnee food storage might have overrun some readers' appetite for detail: "They tried not to open [caches] when it snowed or rained because the moisture would rot the dried corn and squash and the jerked meats."

Mitchell touched on multiple facets of fieldwork throughout the series. Perhaps echoing Boas, he dwelt upon limited financial support for anthropology and wrote appreciatively of those who, prioritizing research over comfort, "eat scantily and live simply, spending every possible copper on the problem." He described the more immersive and overtly participatory quality of Fortune's fieldwork in Dobu. Irony and contingency are leitmotifs throughout. Mitchell reported Benedict's remarks on the exotic norms (dress clothes, first class passage) imposed by English colonial administrators on field-bound American anthropologists. Subjects' reactions to anthropology and anthropologists are a recurring topic. Extrapolating from Alexander Goldenweiser's remarks, Mitchell wrote that "The Indian who does not know a little about the ways [i.e., academic agendas] of the white man is apt to think that the inquisitive anthropologist is a screwball." For an anthropology of an age that accorded no value to local claims of proprietary custom or knowledge, resistance was sometimes an obstacle: Mitchell reported Herzog's difficulties recording songs from Puebloan consultants. He was also attuned to anthropologists' sometimes unexpected recreational and novelty value. Driving back to a Mandan community on Fort Berthold Reservation late one night, Edward Kennard lost his muffler:

> The loud explosive exhaust noises woke up the whole village and Indians came running from all the huts. Dr. Kennard thought they would be extremely angry, but they were pleased by the noise. They made him drive up and down the road … Then they had a ceremony and gave him a tribal name, "Night Hawk."

Mitchell later wrote that, "graveyard humor is an exemplification of the way I look at the world." He ended the series by quoting Benedict's noir observation on mortality and ethnographic completion:

"Usually he [ethnographer] hates to leave a primitive society, feeling that things might turn up in one more week or one more month which could make his study far more valuable ... I am sure there have been times when anthropologists, hating to leave without obtaining authentic data on funeral rituals, have yearned for a death in the tribe."

## Joseph Mitchell and Anthropology

The most astute commentators on Mitchell's journalism have noted affinities with anthropology. Norman Sims, who interviewed Mitchell in 1989, describes his writing "as a web of reporting, cultural anthropology, symbolism, and memoir." Dan Frank, Pantheon Books editor-in-chief, is responsible for publication in 1992 of *Up in the Old Hotel*, the compilation of Mitchell's *New Yorker* writing. For Frank, "Joe's perspective was one remarkably akin to an anthropologist's." Mitchell's 1943 collection *McSorley's Wonderful Saloon* appeared with the Library of Congress subject heading "New York—Social life and customs."

Mitchell remembered the Boas interview as personally and professionally transformative, likening its effects to "being born again." Kunkel calls the encounter "a career-altering revelation." Lines might then be traced between the anthropology series in 1937 and the ethnographic sensibility of Mitchell's later writing. The exact character of the rebirth or revelation, however, still wants elucidation. The anthropology series was followed one year later by Mitchell's employment at *The New Yorker*, complicating the already fraught expedient of discovering before/after transitions in style and subject matter.

*Exoticisms and Alterities*

Anthropology shares with Mitchell's journalism preoccupations with exoticism and difference. It might then be argued that Mitchell's exposure to indigenous alterities via the anthropology series played some formative part in shaping a predilection for their cosmopolitan and metropolitan counterparts. Bailey, for example, identifies Boas' advice as contributory not only to his transition from reporter to literary artist but also his capacity to describe "singular specimens of humanity with compassion and deep, hard-earned understanding."

In the most general terms, New York City itself was an ethnographic field site for the Robeson County, North Carolina-born Mitchell: "I had," he wrote in *My Ears Are Bent,* "a [journalists'] police card in my pocket and I was twenty-one years old and everything was new to me." It was not, however, the New York of the Empire State Building or Fiorello LaGuardia or the Yankees or Broadway theater that engaged Mitchell's journalism. Mitchell, in David Remnick's understated appraisal, "was not much interested in the good and the great." In an autobiographical fragment published in *The New Yorker* Mitchell recalled:

> the pasts of a score or so of strange men and women—bohemians, visionaries, obsessives, impostors, fanatics, lost souls, gypsy kings and gypsy queens, and out-and-out freak-show freaks—whom I got to know and kept in touch with for years while working as a newspaper reporter and whom I thought of back then as being uniquely strange, only-one-of-a-kind-in-the-whole-world strange, but whom, since almost everybody has come to seem strange to me, including myself, I now think of,

without taking a thing away from them, as being strange all right, no doubt about that, but also as being stereotypes—as being stereotypically strange, so to speak, or perhaps prototypically strange would be more exact or archetypically strange or even ur-strange or maybe old-fashioned pre-Freudian-insight strange would be about right.

The closest connections in Mitchell's writing with anthropology's then-signature focus on non-Western peoples are the two Romani pieces, "King of the Gypsies" and "The Gypsy Women," and "The Mohawks in High Steel." In "The Gypsy Women," Mitchell has Detective Daniel J. Campion complain that:

> When I read about American professors studying strange tribes of people in the far corners of the earth, it burns me up; you'd think at least one of them would study a strange tribe that's right under their noses.

Mitchell's long-term interest in Romani is attested by his membership in England's Gypsy Lore Society, including service on its Board of Directors.

For the rest, Mitchell focused on cosmopolitans of more conventionally "Western" provenance. His 1943 book *McSorley's Wonderful Saloon* collected *New Yorker* pieces on, among others, the denizens of the titular saloon, Village celebrity Joseph Gould, Bowery philanthropist Mazie, Broadway mendicant Commodore Dutch, Captain Charlie of the Private Museum for Intelligent People, Calypso singer Wilmoth Houdini, the Union League of the Deaf, biracial child prodigy Phylippa Schuyler, the troglodytic Hollmans of Central Park, and circus performer Jane Barnell, a bearded woman. The book was also indexed, not altogether inappropriately, under the Library of Congress heading "Eccentrics and Eccentricities."

Not all of Mitchell's subjects, however, exhibited marked "strangeness," and such expressions as "lowlife," "eccentric," and "curiosity" circumscribe a more heterogeneous repertoire. Romani, circus freaks, and bohemians notwithstanding, Mitchell also wrote of people less exotic or odd than obscure and journalistically unsung: those, for example, who caught and bought and sold seafood from the waters environing New York. The anthropology series itself attests interest in people consecrated to an obscure profession. Nor were all of Mitchell's subjects "underdogs"—although privileged socio-economic position is rare among them. The Boasian "cosmographic" unity linking exoticism to more prosaic obscurities wants elucidation.

Mitchell's affinity for these outlier subjects long preceded both the anthropology series and employment at *The New Yorker*. An autobiographical fragment from *The New Yorker* recalls the juvenile Mitchell's covert, arboreal surveillance of sharecroppers near his home. Reflecting back later in life, Mitchell traced his connections with such subjects to his years as a reporter from 1930 to 1938. Mitchell's brief career with the *Herald Tribune* (1930-1931) began with a baptism-by-fire assignment to Harlem. Here, Kunkel writes, "He quickly found his way to many of Harlem's more established eccentrics, every one of whom he filed away." His first *New Yorker* story in 1933 was a "Reporter at Large" piece on an Elkton, Maryland quickie-marriage facility serviceable alike to social register couples and carnival employees. Mitchell's work at *The World-Telegram* attests versatile attention both to celebrity profiles and, not unexpectedly, "the city's curiosities." Certain of the latter—Maisie, Commodore Dutch, Phylippa Schuyler—returned in longer *New Yorker* profiles after 1938. As Kunkel observes, a "near obsession, cultivated over a decade pounding pavement for newspapers, with the city's 'lowlife'" was already in place. Mitchell's interests in difference led to the meeting with Boas, not the other way around.

## Cultural Surrounds

The noun "culture" appears in Mitchell's *World-Telegram* series with expectable Boasian plural-and-relative senses: "the Ojibwa culture," "Mandan language and culture." "Culture" does not occur with this meaning in Mitchell's later writing. In "The Mohawks in High Steel," for example, we find such phrases as "Mohawk customs" but not "Caughnawaga culture" or "culture of the Iroquois." Lexical choices aside, a second proposed anthropological influence on Mitchell is the positioning of subjects in their social and cultural surrounds. In his review of *McSorley's Wonderful Saloon*, Malcolm Cowley wrote that Mitchell commonly situated people in "the customs of a whole community." Dan Frank, in dialogue with Kunkel, said similarly that Mitchell's characters existed "in a context, a community, a history, a past that was larger than them, so that one could see how they were shaped, from whence their outlooks and attitudes came." Kunkel explicitly attaches these practices to anthropology, stating that Mitchell acquired from Boas "a clear anthropological approach to understanding his subjects as members of distinct communities with their own values, histories, and prejudices." He describes

"King of the Gypsies" in 1942 as Mitchell's "first true effort at profiling an entire culture," and writes that anthropology afforded Mitchell new insights into his "characters' fundamental motivations," into "why people are who they are and do what they do."

There exists, however, evidence for implicit plural-and-relative cultural sensibilities in Mitchell's work prior to his anthropological encounter. In 1936, Mitchell wrote a short *New Yorker* piece about a place called Dick's Bar and Grill, reprinted as "Bar and Grill" in *My Ears Are Bent*. In 1939, an expanded version appeared in *The New Yorker* as "Obituary of a Gin Mill." In both earlier and later versions, the subject is the anarchic but patterned customs of the place—"a dirty, lawless, back-street gin mill" on the Lower West Side—as animated in and by the proprietors and patrons.

> In the old saloon people were always slugging away at each other. The only rule of behavior Dick [the owner] ever tried to enforce was "No fights outside on the street. It don't look nice. I don't want my store to get a bad name."

So also with "The Old House at Home" in 1940, Mitchells' celebrated historical ethnography of the very different culture of McSorley's Old Ale House.

Mitchell wrote both about individuals and communities, moving reversibly between generalities and particulars. In this respect, his sensibility accords more closely with Edward Sapir than with the individuals he interviewed at Columbia. While open to cultural generalization—he wrote in "King of the Gypsies" that "Gypsies try to make their flats look as much like the inside of a tent as possible"—Mitchell was temperamentally and intellectually immune to Leviathanological determinisms. His accounts to Norman Sims of his own interview techniques and objectives are (expectedly) far from straightforward but privilege biography over culture or community as formative of those "inner selves" his subjects obliquely disclosed in their talk.

### Journalistic Facts and Fictions

The extraordinary literary gifts Mitchell brought to an increasingly ethnographic journalism evoke the venerable question of what anthropology and literature have to do with each other. Mitchell's writing practices evoke dialogues and dialectics shared by anthropology and journalism. Each profession engages questions of how and whether to site boundaries between ethnographic or journalistic representation and fictional invention. In question is the appropriateness of contriving composites and rearrangements of real persons and events or—in the extreme case—devising non-real persons and events.

As Norman Sims shows in *True Stories: A Century of Literary Journalism*, New Journalism(s) of the 1960s were attacked one decade later precisely on grounds of fictional inventions and embellishments. In anthropology parallel conversations derive proximately from the 1980s "writing culture moment," most specifically from James Clifford's assertion in his introduction to *Writing Culture* that ethnographies are fictions—"constructed truths ... made possible by powerful 'lies' of exclusion or rhetoric." Some popular (mis-)readings dismissed alike the possibility and the desirability of distinguishing fieldwork experiences from invented and imagined fictions. The same period saw debates about such ethnographic improvisations, disclosed or otherwise, as composite consultants, discourses, and events; see, for example, Kaminsky on Barbara Myerhoff's *Remembered Lives.*

Mitchell, commonly included among New Journalism ancestors, wrote both fiction and nonfiction, and is known also as a pioneer of experimental mixtures. Mitchell's popular Mr. Flood of the Fulton Fish Market appeared in three mid-1940s *New Yorker* profiles as a biographical personage but was later revealed by the author as a composite when the stories were republished together in 1948 as *Old Mr. Flood.* Kunkel's biography of Mitchell describes further artifice. Two other memorable subjects, each in "chief informant" position, were also composites: Cockeye Johnny Nikanov in "King of the Gypsies" and Orvis Diabo in "The Mohawks in High Steel." In other stories, Mitchell sometimes redistributed persons and events through time and space, and wove into unitary monologues speech heard on separate occasions.

Relations of Mitchell's improvisations to journalistic norms in the 1940s remain unclear. Composite characters and fact-fiction blends clearly flourished at *The New Yorker* on Ross' editorial watch. But the newer revelations in Kunkel's biography highlight fact/fiction fault lines in contemporary journalism. Michael Rosenwald and Michelle Dean exemplify readers from whom these disclosures elicit censure or disillusionment. Kunkel himself describes Mitchell as "bending the boundaries of nonfiction to the point where these particular stories were more accurately fact-based fiction" and imputes to Mitchell himself ambivalence about subordinating journalistic principle to literary ends.

Others celebrate Mitchell's mixtures and improvisations. Norman Sims describes Mitchell's blends as "creative mystery" and writes that it was "along that edge of uncertainty that Mitchell's work soared toward greatness." In Kunkel's biography, editor Dan Frank says, "Yes, there was something literary or artificial in Joe's descriptions. But that did not make his portraits less faithful." Frank sees Mitchell's reshaping of subjects' speech as paradoxical means to superior portrayals of their uniqueness. For Frank, Mitchell's subjects are opposites of fictional characters inspired by worldly originals: They are real people portrayed with a novelist's "imagination, depth, and complexity." The implicit—and ethnography-relevant—alternative is, perhaps, journalism as oral history, with speech literally preserved, performance errors inviolate, in narrow phonetic transcription. Janet Malcolm, Mitchell's friend and colleague at *The New Yorker*, herself a veteran of journalistic invention charges, writes recently that "Mitchell's travels across the line that separates fiction and nonfiction are his singular feat," and that his "genre is some kind of hybrid, as yet to be named."

Mitchell himself expressed varying positions on the question. In the preface to *Old Mr. Flood*, Mitchell wrote, "I wanted these stories to be truthful rather than factual, but they are solidly based on facts." This Zen observation seems to identify in persons and events built from factual prototypes a "truth" absent alike from the unworked originals and from entirely imagined fictions. In interviews with Norman Sims, Mitchell privileged instead a "truth" made of the best possible selections from a thick factual corpus. Of *Joe Gould's Secret*, his last book, Mitchell wrote:

Everything in the Gould book is documented, all those things in *The Dial* and all the records of his family. But I could have used this documentation in a different way. The creative aspect of it is the particularity of the facts that you choose, and the particularity of the conversations that you choose, and the fact that you stayed with the man long enough to get a panoply of conversations from which you can choose the ones that you decide are the most significant. The Gould I described, I think, is the absolutely true Gould. But another person could have written the story about Joe Gould far differently.

The better truths are made from invention and embellishment or from strategic inclusions and exclusions. Unworked factual documentation may obscure truth, a complaint sometimes leveled at Boasian textual practices.

*Literary Ethnographies*

The excellence of Mitchell's journalism evokes also anthropological debates on the ethnographic uses of literature. By the early 1920s, some anthropologists were speculating that literary fiction might be superior to academic prose genres as a means of representing other peoples' customs and, especially, as Alfred Kroeber emphasized, their subjectivities. Consider for example, Franz Boas' "An Eskimo Winter:"

He [Pakkak, a shaman] addressed himself to Attina and said, "Have you sinned? Have you eaten forbidden food? Have you done forbidden work? What taboos have you transgressed?" She had asked herself what she might have done to bring about her child's sickness, and she remembered that she had scraped the frost from the window of her house, and that she had eaten seal meat and caribou meat on the same day.

Sadly not broached in the Mitchell-Boas interview, this experiment was among twenty-three ethnographic fictions assembled by Elsie Clews Parsons in the 1922 collection *American Indian Life*. In his review of this book in *The Dial*, Joseph Gould's preferred forum, Edward Sapir asked,

> To what extent can we penetrate into the vitals of primitive life and fashion for ourselves satisfying pictures on its own level of reality? Can the conscious knowledge of the ethnologist be fused with the intuitions of the artist?

Sapir pronounced favorably, overall, on the viability and promise of such fusions.

Decades later, in the 1980s, questions of literature's ethnographic utility re-emerged in the form of experiments with fiction and literary nonfiction as proposed remedies to the default ethnographic realism.

In affirming the value of Mitchell's improvisations, Janet Malcolm proposed that journalistic norms against "bending actuality to our artistic will" are, in the first instance, born of incapacity rather than principle (and thus a necessity become virtue?):

> Reporters don't invent because they don't know how to. This is why they are journalists rather than novelists or short-story writers ... They couldn't create a character like Mr. Flood or Cockeye Johnny if you held a gun to their heads.

Malcolm effectively rattled her targeted cages. Dean reports, for example, that New York University journalism professor Mitchell Stephens called Malcolm's argument "scary" and "obnoxious."

The fact that most reporters "don't know how" creatively to invent does not, of course, stop some from trying. And so also with anthropologists. Kirin Narayan's writing on Chekhov's *Sakhalin Island* demonstrates twice over the value of literary nonfiction for ethnography and anthropology. Similar conclusions might be reached for some ethnographic fiction. These and other exceptions notwithstanding, Malcolm's remarks invite comparison with Sapir whose affirmation of fiction's value was qualified by observations that most contributors to *American Indian Life* couldn't write their way out of a paper bag. In 2016, as in the 1920s, those who encourage anthropologists—or other academics—to experiment with literary techniques may sooner or later be confronted with the prospect of reading the results.

*Fieldwork and Talk*

Although he could return home each night, Mitchell's investigative practices parallel anthropological fieldwork in certain respects, notably protracted, repeated, and immersive presence in subjects' milieus. His research was commonly observational and often overtly participatory: he attended an East Side "beefsteak," participated in Commodore Dutch's annual ball, and logged strenuous nights with Joe Gould in Village bars. Mitchell may have analogized the ethnographic interviews described by anthropologists to his own journalistic experience. His writing famously exhibits attentiveness to fine details of what is done and said. His journalism shares with anthropology—most specifically with the "life history" genre—appreciation for the uses of memory and speech. He was thus unsurprisingly intrigued by the feats and capacities of Gene Weltfish's Pawnee consultant Mark Evarts:

> Once he [Evarts] listed 128 men by name who could have been invited to a certain feast, and then told me how many were invited. Then he told me why those who could have been invited were not. This was a feast that took place forty or fifty years ago.

Mitchell shared this proclivity for talk with his most famous subject, Joseph Ferdinand Gould. Likeness between them has long been noted, not least by Mitchell himself. As he told Sims, "God forgive me for my version of Flaubert's remark about Madame Bovary." (It is of passing interest that, as Jill LePore shows, Gould in the 1910s "once tried to recruit Franz Boas for a campaign he was waging to aid Albania. 'I think we have seen sufficiently clearly what that kind of 'help' leads to,' Boas wrote back. Then he dropped the correspondence.") Mitchell and Gould each took uncommon specimens as preferred subjects and accorded surpassing value to their speech. Gould's mysterious book *The Oral History of Our Time* purportedly contained paraphrases and verbatim transcriptions of overheard conversations from different downtown demimondes. Mitchell famously used lengthy passages of quoted, monologic speech to tell his and his subjects' stories.

Mitchell's *New Yorker* colleague Stanley Hyman was perhaps the first to register the resemblance of Gould's oral history to Mitchell's journalism:

"Finally we realize that the body of Mitchell's work is precisely that Oral History of Our Time that Gould himself could not write." In *Joe Gould's Secret* in 1964, Mitchell disclosed his conclusion that Gould's oral history book did not exist. Since 1965, dispersed Gould-authored texts of heterogeneous kind have periodically surfaced. On the basis of interviews and newer archival findings, Jill LePore shows that fragments of oral history writing by Gould do, indeed, exist.

## Documentation, Preservation, Nostalgia

Boasian anthropology's commitment to documentation of pre-European Native American societies found a parallel in Mitchell's dedication to notionally anachronistic peoples, places, and practices in New York City. In 1943 Malcolm Cowley wrote of "King of the Gypsies" that it:

> sets out to describe Cockeye Johnny Nikanov, the spokesman or king of thirty-eight gypsy families, but it soon becomes a Gibbon's decline and fall of the American gypsies.

If Mitchell's journalism prioritized documentation, he also actively pursued preservationist agendas. As an older New York City fell around him, Mitchell became an active member of the Society of Architectural Historians, the Society of Industrial Archaeology, the Friends of Cast Iron Architecture, and the South Street Seaport Museum. From 1982 to 1987 he was a Commissioner of the New York City Landmarks Preservation Commission.

## "Don't take anything for granted"

Boasian anthropology sometimes problematized the superiority of "civilized" societies over "primitive" counterparts. Mitchell independently developed early in his career a parallel perspective on his own subjects. He remembered that Boas began telling him "how to look at the world," instructing him not to "take anything for granted." Mitchell's somewhat elliptical example concerned drinking stories. Boas, he said, led him to question the value of drinking as journalistic topic—and perhaps also as recreation. This in turn inspired awareness of incongruity between such "dubious" subject matter and his own literary potential. This insight, if such it was, had no lasting influence. After joining *The New Yorker* in 1938, Mitchell continued writing about drinkers and drinking, notably "The Old House at Home" about McSorley's Old Ale House.

Boas' admonition "don't take anything for granted," with its connotations of defamiliarization, doubtless had other and more significant influences on dispositions Mitchell carried with him to New York and cultivated there. Principal among these was skepticism—or outright antipathy—to class, race, and ethnicity, and also to physical and psychological normalcy as criteria for according value, whether to journalistic subjects in particular or to people in general. Ignoring "the good and the great," Mitchell's *New Yorker* writing promoted uncommon specimens of the common man as privileged subjects. Mitchell's friends and *New Yorker* colleagues A.J. Liebling and John McNulty, and perhaps others, shared this iconoclasm—as did their readers. Sims repeats Mitchell's account of how *New Yorker* editor Harold Ross finessed this inversionary reordering of "lowlife" over "highlife" profiles.

These inversions did not go unnoticed in reviews of Mitchell's 1943 book *McSorley's Wonderful Saloon*. A *Time Magazine* reviewer quoted by Kunkel observed fastidiously of Mitchell and his subjects that "For years he has been studying, with the prying patience of a botanist, the queer human weeds he finds growing in the dingier interstices of Manhattan's bum-littered Bowery." Mitchell had anticipated such reactions in an author's note:

> The people in a number of the stories are of a kind that many writers have got in the habit of referring to as "little people." I regard this phrase as patronizing and repulsive. There are no little people in this book. They are as big as you are, whoever you are.

Anthropology did not originate Mitchell's appreciation for alterity or his attentiveness to social surrounds—but it plausibly quickened a sensibility where these were already deeply felt. The encounter in 1937 with Boas and his colleagues might well, in Edmund Wilson-speak, have afforded Mitchell an intertextual "shock of recognition."

## Acknowledgments

Sometime in the mid-2000s Marshall Sahlins proposed locating Joseph Mitchell's anthropology interviews and reprinting them as a Prickly Paradigm pamphlet; he also provided valuable editorial inputs. Mitchell's biographer Thomas Kunkel provided the dates of the six *New York World-Telegram* installments. Dan Frank, Editor-in-Chief of Pantheon Books, was generous with information and encouragement. Maria Lepowsky provided photocopies of Mitchell's anthropology series from microfilm copies in the Wisconsin Historical Society Newspaper Collections. Earle E. Spamer, Reference Archivist at The American Philosophical Society, located correspondence in the Franz Boas Papers. Nora Sanborn, Joseph Mitchell's daughter, generously encouraged the project. Matthew Knisley typed the manuscript from copies of the *New York World-Telegram* series.

## Notice

Sources referred to in this introduction are posted as a PDF on the Prickly Paradigm Press website at http://www.prickly-paradigm.com.

*New York World-Telegram*
1937

# Man—With Variations

## Anthropologists Smile as Hitler Talks of His "Pure Germany"

*The first of a series of articles on the battle of anthropologists to know man, from the primitive to the modern, before the evidence is lost. The cold answer of science to Hitler.*

By JOSEPH MITCHELL
*World-Telegram Staff Writer*

The number of primitives uninfluenced by contact with such products of Western civilization as plug tobacco, the Holy Bible, radio programs, pants, hangovers, pinball games, toothpaste, and Joe E. Brown is swiftly diminishing. At this instant, hampered by an insufficient supply of cold cash, scores of energetic anthropologists from American universities and museums are trying their best to examine all remaining pristine societies before they are warped by the missionary and the businessman.

The anthropologist, however, does not lose interest in a society merely because it is no longer truly primitive. He is just as interested in the habits of the reservation Indian who, perhaps, eats corn flakes for breakfast and believes firmly in the Townsend plan, as he is in the dour, anti-social Dobuan who lives by sorcery and believes that the yams in his garden emerge from the ground at night and roam the bush tracks, returning to their holes before daybreak. He is just as interested in the physical changes in the descendants of immigrants, or in their motor habits (the sweeping, symbolic gestures of the first-generation Italian, for instance, as contrasted with the jerky gestures of the first generation Jew), as he is in the felicitous sexual life of the Trobriands or the ghost dance trances of the Pawnees.

## GREAT DEAL MORE.

A great deal more is involved in anthropology, however, than collecting weird facts about the customs and notions of the higher mammal. The frivolous, impotent curiosity of the believe-it-or-not cartoonist does not motivate the anthropologist who undergoes months of discomfort in order to learn, for example, that the pickle-puss is respected among the Dobuans, whose conventions ban laughter, or that there was until a few years ago a suicidal insanity rampant among the Ojibwe in Ontario, an insanity in which victims begged to be burned to death and in later stages became canni-balistic, believing persons around them to be beavers and trying to eat them.

Stated simply, anthropology is the study of man as he lives in social groups, and it embraces a whole array of sciences. When an anthropologist goes to study the sorcery carried on in the yam patches of the mutually treacherous Dobuans, or when he digs into the memory of the Pawnee to find out how the ghost dance was spawned, or when he measures the skulls of the immigrants, he is, actually, in the words of Dr. Franz Boas, trying to discover "whether any generally valid laws exist that govern the life of society." Dr. Boas believes that "almost every anthropological problem touches our most intimate life."

## ANALYTIC WORLD.

"The course of development of a group of children depends upon their racial descent, the economic condition of their parents and their general well-being," Dr. Boas once wrote. "A knowledge of the interaction of these factors may give us the power to control growth and to secure the best possible conditions of life for the group."

## WHAT IS RACE.

At this moment information gathered tediously in hundreds of obscure cultures—the rich background of anthropology—is forcing such scientists as philosophers of law, psychologists, sociologists, psychoanalysts and economists to reevaluate their concepts. Many of the laws and principles of these sciences are based entirely on data drawn from our own, or Western, civilization, and it is wrongly assumed that they hold true for human conditions wherever found; many of them, as a matter of fact, break down when checked against the discoveries of anthropologists. The concept of instincts is an example. After examining the work of such persons as Boas, Malinowski, Sapir, Herskovits, Lowie, Benedict, Mead and Fortune, no psychologist will ever again be dogmatic about such things as "instinct" of acquisitiveness, or the "instinct" of mother love.

The relation of facts about primitive environments to our own steam-heated environment may seem obscure at first, but when one remembers that the anthropologist is preoccupied with the study of races and reflects on the damage done in our time by stress on "racial purity" and "racial characteristics" it is no longer obscure. The insistence on a "pure Germany" by that noble Austrian, Adolf Hitler, and the amazing German racial laws of 1935 are enormously funny and enormously tragic to anthropologists. When Julius Streicher cries that "blood cells of Jews differ greatly from those of Nordics," the anthropologist does not know whether to snicker or to weep.

Faced with these matters Dr. Boas, for example, is forced to reflect that "the world is sick." Dr. Boas knows that the term "race" is vague and approximate, and that there is no such thing as a "pure race," and he doubts if there is any "superior race." He knows that the anatomist cannot tell the difference between the brains of a Swede and a Negro. He believes that "if we were to select the most intelligent, imaginative, energetic and emotionally stable third of mankind, all races would be represented."

The idea that Dr. Boas has about race may be summed up within a few paragraphs. They are:—

"The term 'race' is meant to indicate individuals of common ancestry and similar bodily form."

## SOME MISNOMERS.

"In the United States it has become customary to use the term race instead of nationality. Immigration authorities speak of Italian, Polish, German races and so on. Since citizens of any one of these nationalities are neither of the same ancestry nor of the same bodily form, the use of the term "race" is inappropriate ... The terms Anglo-Saxon, Slavic, Latin, Aryan race are equally inappropriate since they designate people speaking certain languages without any reference to their ancestry or bodily form.

Languages are acquired by people of the most diverse descent.

"The nearest approach to a group corresponding to what is appropriately called a local race or type is found in populations of small districts in which a group of families has lived and intermarried for a long time, so that all the living members have more or less a common ancestry.

"The more alike the bodily forms of these ancestors the more homogenous will be the group. The origin of fundamentally distinct races like Negroes and whites springs from the fact that these groups became isolated in very early times, sufficiently remote to permit the rise of far-reaching differences in bodily form. With the increasing number of human beings, the isolation of small groups ceased. They came into contact, intermarried, and the forms in each group became more diversified. These migrations and intermixtures have continued for many thousand years. In Europe, Western Asia, and North Africa particularly, no people exist that can derive its ancestry from a single source. The populations of this area are so much alike that the assignment of an individual, on the basis of his bodily appearance, to his proper local group is never quite certain, often impossible.

## FAMILY STRAINS.

"On account of the diversity of family strains in a population, it is impossible to speak of racial heredity except in regard to such general traits as differentiate whites, Negroes and Mongols, and which are common to all members of these racial groups. We can study hereditary form and behavior only in family lines.

"No proof has even been given showing that bodily form, as expressed in hair color, form of head, face, nose, or stature determines in any way behavior. On the contrary it can be proven that behavior is constantly changing with changing conditions. (Here Dr. Boas points out that the types of crimes committed by descendants of immigrants tend to change in American urban environment to the types characteristic of American cities.)

"The facts here set forth prove the following points:—The assumption of the biological homogeneity of any race is a fiction. Every race contains many family strains which are biologically distinct and most of which are found in varying number in races as closely related as varieties of the white race. The physiological and psychological behavior of the individuals depends only in part upon his hereditary characteristics. These differ widely within every population and are strongly overlaid by outer, cultural influences which modify the hereditary traits. It is, therefore, impossible to countenance the theory that descent from a fictitious uniform race determines the character of a whole people."

The foregoing quotations help to explain why books by Dr. Boas, unquestionably the greatest anthropologist in the world, who is a native of Minden, in Westphalia, were thrown, after the Nazi ascendancy, into a "book bonfire" in a square before the University of Kiel, his alma mater, a university whose officials a few years earlier tried to think of some honor which the distinguished doctor had not already received and finally gave him an honorary M.D.

—

*Tomorrow:—Dr. Boas and the men he trained.*

—

*New York World-Telegram*
1937

# Man—With Variations

## Enormously Learned Dr. Boas, Outstanding Anthropologist, at 78 Is Most Dangerous Foe of Hitler's Racial Concepts

*The second of a series of articles on the race among or by anthropologists to know man, from the primitive to the modern, before the evidence is lost. The cold answer of science to Hitler.*

By JOSEPH MITCHELL
*World-Telegram Staff Writer*

If logic meant anything at all in this world of sorrow, the most dangerous enemy of Adolf Hitler's racial concepts—his Aryan clause and his weird classification of citizens—would be a stern, enormously learned old man.

Now 78, and retired, with piercing eyes and a thinning shock of scraggy white hair, he works almost every day behind a door in Schermerhorn Extension at Columbia University on which is lettered, "Research Laboratory. F. Boas." Of all the scientists in the world, Dr. Franz Boas is best fitted to evaluate the Nazi ideas of race. He has one word for them—"Nonsense."

Scientists are always pained by the illogical, and the Nazi ideas are particularly painful to Dr. Boas. More than a quarter of a century ago, he disproved concepts of race similar to those firmly held at present by the Reichsfuehrer and his disciples.

He thought the matter was settled long ago, and now, contrary to all logic, the same trouble-making concepts have popped up again.

In his busy years as an anthropologist Dr. Boas has done work of great importance in virtually every branch of the science—linguistics, primitive mentality, folklore, ethnology, growth and senility, the physical effects of environment—and he is by no means finished with what he started fifty-six years ago.

With so much to be done in anthropology, it irks him when he is obliged to waste time with things so preposterous as Aryanism.

## HARD TO INTERVIEW.

In influence and in the volume of significant work he has turned out, Dr. Boas is the most influential anthropologist in the world. He has trained practically every great anthropologist in the United States; the heads of departments of anthropology in almost every major American university—at Northwestern, Chicago, Yale, California, and Wisconsin—sat under Boas at one time or another.

However, when Dr. Boas retired from active service at Columbia last summer, after forty-one years as professor and lecturer, reporters found it hard to gather enough personal information about him to write the stories customary in such cases.

Always difficult to interview, personal publicity and the popularization of his theories and findings have always been repugnant to him. However, since his retirement he has been friendlier to reporters, delighting them by muttering in a thick German accent such words as "nonsense" or "preposterous" when asked to comment on some statement or other by a Nazi propagandist.

He is not always angry about such things, however; it is not easy to forget the sadness in his voice when, asked about the bonfire made of his books by students at Kiel, his alma mater, he said:—

"If people want to be crazy, what can you do about it?"

A few years ago he wrote "Anthropology and Modern Life," which can be read with a minimum of pain by laymen. Recently, also, many facts about his life have been made public by his students, most of whom call him "Papa Franz."

He was born in Minden, Westphalia, of German Jew parents. Educated at the universities of Heidelberg, Bonn and Kiel, he received his doctorate from Kiel in 1881. He started as a physicist, but an itch to travel and a liking for geography swerved him toward anthropology.

Soon after receiving his Ph.D. he felt the urge to go to Greenland on a ship which was to bring back a party of meteorologists. When his father refused to put up the cash for the trip, he financed it himself, finally by, of all things, contracting to write a series of travel articles for a newspaper.

When he reached Baffin Land he became interested in the Central Eskimo, unpacked his bags, and stayed for the better part of the years 1883 and 1884. He returned to Germany with material on the geography of the icy region, an enormous amount of data on the cultural life of the Central Eskimo and an ethnographical collection of specimens. He finished a book about them, became an anthropologist.

## VACATIONED IN THE FIELD.

A few years later he came to the United States to marry Marie Krackowizer, daughter of a famous Austrian surgeon, who died a few years ago. Soon he began field work among the Indians of the North Pacific Coast of North America, work which is still in progress.

His first teaching job here was with Clark University, a job he left to prepare the first scientific exhibition of American ethnology for the Chicago World's Fair of 1893. This exhibition was not as popular as the mild hip-wriggling of Mrs. Andrew Spyropolous, the Little Egypt, who died recently, but that did not dismay Dr. Boas.

In 1895 he began to teach at Columbia, and soon amazed other professors by stating flatly that some students his own renown was attracting had no business to be anthropologists. During the summers he worked on the North Pacific coast, in Puerto Rico, Mexico and in the Southwest pueblos. Like most anthropologists, he spent his sabbatical terms in the field.

In 1931, for example, when elected to the presidency of the American Assn. for the Advancement of Science, he was visiting with the Kwakiutl Indians of Vancouver Island, the tribe with which he has been most closely identified. His Indian grammars, and his studies of Indian art, music and religion are respected all over the world. Experts regard his "Tsimshian Mythology" as a classic concordance of North American myths.

# SUCCEEDED BY WOMAN.

Under Dr. Boas the anthropology department at Columbia became one of the finest in the world. His students went into the field early, and some were field-trip veterans before they reached 30. He has never had enough money to go around, however, although an anthropological expedition is comparatively inexpensive (a summer's work in a North American Indian tribe will cost not much more than $500; a year's study in South America will come to $3,000, and anthropologists have carried out one year's work in Africa and Melanesia for $4,000).

Columbia anthropologists lead in field work in the United States. At one period in 1936, for instance, Martha Champion was studying the music of the Iroquois; Buell Quain was in Vanua Levu, Fiji; William Whitman was working on the social organization of the San Ildefonso Pueblo of New Mexico; William Lipkind was preparing a linguistic study of the Winnebago Indians of the Plains; Edward Kennard was working among the Hopi; Ruth Landes was with the Potawatomi of Nebraska; Marian Smith was with the Puyalup of Puget Sound; Henry Elkin was with the Arapaho Indians of the Plains; Marvin Opler was with the Ute in Colorado; Gordon Marsh was with the Iowa, studying their language; Charles Wagley was digging among Indian mounds near Macon, Ga., with the help of 250 WPA workers; and Reo Fortune was in New Guinea.

Since the retirement from active duty of Dr. Boas, Dr. Ruth Benedict has been acting executive officer of the department. She is an erect, handsome, prematurely white-haired woman. One of the most brilliant of American theoreticians, she has been especially interested in the psychological aspects of anthropology.

Dr. Benedict once wrote a tabloid evaluation of the work of Dr. Boas, which, while technically worded, is clear enough for appreciation by the layman.

"In his work in physical anthropology," she wrote, "he has constantly called attention to the necessity of investigations into the rates and processes of physical change so that we may know something of the behavior of physical measurements under various hereditary and environmental conditions, information that is necessary before we can intelligently use physical statistics as a basis for the classification of human groups."

In her first paragraph, Dr. Benedict refers to research which has been dear to the heart of her predecessor. In 1908 the U.S. Immigration and Naturalization Service asked Dr. Boas to study the physical changes in the descendants of immigrants, and he has piled abundant evidence that such changes do occur. He once said, "Just in the same way as the proportions of the body, head and face of animals born in captivity change when compared with their wild-born ancestors, thus the bodily proportions of man undergo minute changes in the new environment."

—

*Tomorrow:—The work and hardships of young scientists in the field.*

—

*New York World-Telegram*
1937

# Man—With Variations

## Average Anthropologist Gets a $500 Grant to Do a Miracle—and He Generally Does, Groping for Ghost of the Past

*Third in a series of articles.*

By JOSEPH MITCHELL
*World-Telegram Staff Writer*

Nothing disgusts the average young anthropologist so much as the heroic stories in the newspapers about those African expeditions organized by well-heeled young gents whose mamas are willing to buy them yachts and tons of Abercrombie & Fitch equipment just to keep them from going on sitdown strikes in fancy gin mills or from getting themselves betrothed to fan dancers.

The anthropologist knows that the young gentlemen, after dedicating their lives to science, according to their quotes in the newspapers, will return in eight or nine months with a gross of flea-bitten snake and lion skins and an album stuck full of candid photographs of the hootchy-koochy dancers of Bali, most of whom use Springtime in Paris perfume, drink gin, eat cornflakes for breakfast and are about as primitive as Mrs. Carrie Chapman Catt. The skins and snakes they bring back might just as well have been ordered from some pet dealer in Cape

Town so far as the advancement of science is concerned.

All this trilling scientific work disgusts the average young anthropologist because he, a trained scientist, usually has to work on a small, tight budget. If, for instance, he goes for a summer's work on aboriginal linguistics he will not have much more than $500 to spend, and he will probably buy a used automobile to save traveling expenses, selling it when he returns and he will eat scantily and live simply, spending every possible copper on the problem he has set for himself.

## SOME WORKERS.

Let us examine work done recently on field trips by a few young anthropologists. Most of them worked with grants received from the department of anthropology at Columbia University or from allied foundations. Most of them are in their twenties. All brought back valuable information.

Take Ruth Landes, Ph.D., for instance. Dr. Landes returned recently from a field trip to the Ojibwa reservation in Ontario, just across the United States border, a trip that lasted nine months. Dr. Landes worked in seven villages, and now is in constant touch with one of her informants, an Indian woman who knows English. It was important to study the Ojibwa culture since little is known about the Algonquin tribes of North America. It was believed that a thoroughgoing account of the Ojibwa would add considerably to knowledge about the Algonquin.

The Ojibwa are individualistic, placing great value on private property. They are hunters. The Canadian government failed in an attempt to teach them agriculture. They hunt moose, caribou, deer and bear, and are adroit trappers. Last year, one Ojibwa realized more than $1,000 from furs he took from his traps.

## RISE OF WOMEN.

Because of the stress the society places on property and individualistic achievement women can rise to powerful positions in the tribe once they demonstrate they are equal in ability with men. Many women are warriors and some have been permitted to lead war parties. At one time female shamans, or medicine women, were plentiful among the Ojibwa, which is unusual in North America. If a woman had visionary power and could back it up by accomplishment in curing divination and by leading dangerous expeditions, her status as shaman was undisputed. As soon as a woman became a shaman, however, she was unsexed and was considered an hermaphrodite.

Until about twelve years ago the Ojibwa were murderously paranoiac. The climate is inhospitable. The winters are long and bitter. Consequently the people suffered from starvation and psychic insecurity. This feeling of insecurity was often manifested in a peculiar insanity in which the deranged became mute and cataleptic. In early stages the sufferer feared they were starving to death, and had hallucinations in which they thought the people around them were beavers. Beavers are edible animals.

The sufferers realized they were undergoing hallucinatory experiences, and begged their relatives to kill them. This was often done. However, it was executed in a ceremonial fashion, and took the form of cremation by certain socially designated relatives. A woman, for example, might ask her brother-in-law to burn her, since between them there was a feeling of intimacy which anthropologists call "a joking relationship." This relationship is contrasted with the taboo status between, for example, a man and his mother-in-law.

The insane were burned because the people believed they were possessed by a certain evil spirit, windigo, which takes the form of a giant cannibal skeleton of ice who lives only during the winter. This ice skeleton symbolizes the untold numbers of Ojibwa who died during winters. The Indians know, of course, that the method of dissipating ice is by melting it with heat. Thus this ceremonial cremation is the approved form of getting rid of the windigo.

If cremation did not take place cannibalism sometimes resulted. In a hunger frenzy an insane Indian would kill someone, usually a child, and eat, believing he was eating a beaver. When the insanity progressed to this phase tribesmen would straitjacket a sufferer, and then let blood from that part of the body considered most infected by windigo. In less advanced cases the insane went on war parties, seeking death. The ceremonial cremations were halted twelve years ago by the Canadian government, but cases of windigo derangement still appear in all Ojibwa villages.

## CHRISTIAN INFLUENCE.

There are seven distinct Ojibwa villages and Dr. Landes was able to check and recheck her material. Some of the tribes studied by anthropologists are just about extinct, however. Such a tribe is the Mandan, which was studied recently by Dr. Edward Kennard. Since they were one of the most important of the Plains tribes at one time, a study of the Mandan language and culture was considered important by anthropologists. The reservation is in North Dakota. When he arrived at the reservation, Dr. Kennard found forty Mandans still living, but only two of these had both parents who were Mandan-speaking. (The tribe originally numbered 1,500, but such afflictions as smallpox and government supervision had reduced them to forty.)

It was difficult to work successfully with these Indians since there were so few of them and since they had all been influenced by Christian missionaries of various denominations since 1880. It was necessary, of course, to eliminate all Christian influences in drawing a correct picture of the aboriginal culture. Dr. Kennard succeeded, however, in obtaining extensive Mandan texts which he subsequently analyzed and published.

He recorded a number of Mandan origin myths. After telling him several origin stories one informant, a shy woman, informed him there was one more story, exceedingly sacred, which she would tell him for $10. Myths are considered personal property by the Mandan, much as a saddle or a bottle of rye is personal property, and belong to those who know them. Dr. Kennard put cash on the line and the woman told the myth laboriously and in great detail. He took it down phonetically in the Mandan language. When he got back to Columbia and translated the myth he found he had paid $10 for a variation of the origin explanation in Genesis, an echo of the days when missionaries lived among the Mandan.

Dr. Kennard lived among the Mandan, going to a North Dakota village for supplies in a dilapidated automobile he had picked up before beginning his trip.

One night he was held up in town and did not get back to the Indian village until past midnight. On the way in he dropped his muffler somewhere in the dust of the road. The loud explosive exhaust noises woke up the whole village and Indians came running from all the huts. Dr. Kennard thought they would be extremely angry, but they were pleased by the noise. They made him drive up and down the road, making more noise than a drunk with a shotgun. Then they had a ceremony and gave him a tribal name, "Night Hawk."

—

*Tomorrow:—Music of the Primitives.*

—

*New York World-Telegram*
1937

# Man—With Variations

## Primitive Music of Aborigines is Preserved for Posterity

*The fourth of a series.*

By JOSEPH MITCHELL
*World-Telegram Staff Writer*

The expensively educated, expensively dressed and expensively fed citizen of Park Ave., who should be, even if he isn't, the finest product of what we are in the habit of referring to as Western civilization, is apt to believe that the music wrenched out of a saxophone, a trumpet and a set of drums by a night club orchestra is "primitive."

The adjectives he has for jazz are "savage," "barbaric" and "primitive." When the rooting and the tooting of a honky-tonk band begins to agitate his aristocratic stomach muscles he is likely to turn to the blonde sweet potato at his elbow and say, "How definitely savage," or, "How too, too primitive" or words to that effect.

This conception of primitive music does not please Dr. George Herzog, a lecturer in the department of anthropology at Columbia University. Dr. Herzog is an authority on the music of primitives. That is his specialty.

Like most anthropologists, Dr. Herzog started out to be something else, but his jump into the field was not as abrupt as the jump made, for example, by Dr. Franz Boas, who was studying the color of sea water immediately before he became an anthropologist. Dr. Herzog started out to be a pianist. He was born in Budapest, and while studying the piano he became interested in Hungarian peasant music. In 1922 he moved on to Berlin, working until 1925 as an assistant of Professor Erich M. von Hornbostel, who recently died in exile and whose musical archives contained 10,000 phonograph records made in primitive societies. In 1925 Dr. Herzog decided to become an anthropologist, and came to Morningside Heights to work under Dr. Boas. Since then he has studied the music of Negroes on the west coast of Africa and about fifteen Indian tribes. He has written a number of highly technical papers, and has gone on field trips on two continents. He has made phonograph records of the music of such Indian tribes as the Sioux, Pueblo, Navajo, Hopi and Pima, and of Negroes in Liberia. Columbia now has a collection of 3,000 records of primitive music, and Dr. Herzog is in charge of them.

## FORMALIZED MUSIC.

"A primitive song is not just a series of grunts and howls, and when a primitive makes music he does not just grab a drum and start hammering on it," said Dr. Herzog. "Primitive music is formalized. Every primitive style is a consistent artistic growth, just like our styles, and has a historical background. Primitive man used and still uses a large variety of musical instruments with special tone colors and timbres."

The drum is perhaps the most important instrument used by primitives, and Dr. Herzog had a lot to say about the importance of the drum in Liberia, the Negro republic of the west coast of Africa.

"The University of Chicago sent me on an expedition to Liberia in 1930," he said. "I went to study the music, and I took with me a young Liberian named Charles G. Blooah, who had been educated in the United States. He ran away from his village with a missionary when he was a child, and had been given up for lost by his people. He was a member of a chief's family and we were well received."

"I was particularly interested in the drum language, or drum signaling. Some explorers have reported that a Negro in the heart of Africa can beat out a message on a drum, and that his message can be picked up and relayed by drummers in other tribes so effectively that soon the message may be known all over the continent."

"That story is melodrama, but the work of the drummers is exceedingly fascinating. The signal drums are made of hollowed-out logs, and syllables, whole words and whole sentences may be beaten out on them. Sometimes a drummer can be heard for twenty miles, beating out a message, but the range is usually no more than three or four miles. A drummer will call all people to the village, telling them about danger, or that a big meeting has been called, or that some large animals have been killed and the meat is to be distributed, or that an important person is dead.

## DRUMMING INSULTS.

"In some places the drumming is nothing but conversation. In the Congo region a man who has an enemy in another village down the river will get into his canoe in the dead of night. He will slip down the river until he is opposite his enemy's village. Then he will get out his drum and hammer out epithets, making all kinds of slurring remarks about his enemy. The whole village will wake up and listen, enjoying the whole thing. When the man in the canoe pauses for a moment his enemy makes a reply, returning epithet for epithet."

"The Liberian government has destroyed hundreds of the drums, in order to promote the success of taxation. When tax collectors appear among the villages, the drummer gives the signal. Then the people vanish into the forest. Everyone simply disappears to evade the hut taxes. They will stay in the woods until the collectors leave. The drums are hard to make. It takes a specialist weeks to turn out one. They are made of hardwood, and are uncovered. Some are six feet long. The dance drums are covered with skins, the skins of monkeys or big lizards or snakes. They may be beaten with the hands or with sticks. I brought one signal drum back with me. It is owned by the University of Chicago."

In the field, Dr. Herzog records songs and music on cylinder records. His equipment is about the size of a picnic hamper. In Liberia he took down dance songs and work songs and songs honoring or praising individuals. Songmakers wander through Liberian villages, picking out important individuals and making songs for them. If they are not paid enough they twist the song a little, make it derisive, the racketeers. Other songs recorded by Dr. Herzog were mourning songs and a curious kind of composition, much like a legal document, in which all the possessions and privileges of a clan are enumerated. These songs become official records of property.

# SINGING THE NEWS.

"Another kind of African song is much like our newspaper," he said. "In Central Africa when something new or funny or unusual happens a song is made of it, and the song lives on until all interest in the happening dies out. For example, if a white man, a hunter, comes into the jungle and shoots at an animal and misses, a song is made about the matter, a song which gleefully recites how the big white hunter took aim, how he shot, how he missed, and how he cursed."

"A song has many functions in a primitive society. Among the Eskimos a song may furnish emotional relief, relief from an irritation. When rivalry threatens to cause an open fight between two men they will get together and stage a song combat instead, in which they revile one another fiercely and thoroughly. The one who has been wittier is declared the winner. More serious clashes are undoubtedly averted by these combats."

The aborigines of the southwest were more difficult to deal with than the west coast Africans, Dr. Herzog found.

"Before an anthropologist goes to study primitive music he gets in touch, if possible, with people who have previously lived in the tribe," he said. Before I started out to see the tribes in the Southwest I interviewed anthropologists who had been in the territory on other missions. I also talked with Indian agents and traders. I got from them the names and dispositions of the best singers. Then I went to these Indians, some of whom were hostile at first, and explained laboriously just what I had in mind. I told them my purpose was to preserve their music, that it was unwritten and in danger of dying out since many songs lingered only in the memories of the oldest men. When an Indian caught on it was sometimes necessary to take him away from the tribe to some secret place. Assured that his confidence would be respected he would dig into his memory for the information I wanted.

## FEARED LOSING SONGS.

Resistance against giving a song was not uncommon. Some were unable to figure out why a white man should be interested in such matters. Other, men who possessed sacred songs, were too frightened at first to sing them. Other felt that if they sang a song into my machine it was gone for good. One aged Indian said, "If you take my song and put it on a record and then the record is broken the song will be lost forever!" Some tribes felt a song was power and that the power would be impaired if a stranger took the song away.

"Also, some songs are personal property. If you achieve a brave deed, for example, a song is made for you and it belongs to you. When your name is mentioned in a meeting you get up and sing it. Other songs are copyrighted. That is, if someone wants to sing your song at a celebration to which you are not going he has to obtain your permission. These songs, of course, were difficult to get."

These entertainment, work and ritual songs, as well as music from the instruments with which they were customarily accompanied—the drums, the deco-rated gourd rattles, the whistles, the sweet flageolet of the plains tribes, the rare musical bow with its fibre string—are now, embalmed in wax, kept for posterity on dusty shelves up at Mr. Nicholas Murray Butler's academy. They will be here when the Indians are long gone.

—

*Tomorrow:—Indian customs and tribal laws.*

—

*New York World-Telegram*
1937

# Man—With Variations

## Aged Pawnee Recalls Laws
## and Rituals of Ancestors

*The fifth of a series.*

By JOSEPH MITCHELL
*World-Telegram Staff Writer*

An apparently limitless amount of information about aboriginal life in Nebraska and Oklahoma is cached in the brain-box of Mark Evarts, an aged, beer-drinking Pawnee. He can talk for solid weeks about the ancient tribal laws, religious rituals, economics, family life and political organizations of the Pawnee. Amazed by his mnemonic feats, anthropologists call him a "walking history" of the Pawnee.

He left the tribe in his youth to became a harness-maker in Harrisburg, Pa., returning in 1897 during the time of the great ghost dances, when the Pawnee went into trances and believed a great storm was coming in which white people would vanish from the earth and in which tremendous herds of buffalo would reappear on the plains.

The ghost dance movement was so strong the United States government made haste to put it down. Evarts recalls the days as a ghost dancer with such clarity that anthropologists are suspicious until they check his conversations against written records—Indian treaties, accounts of travelers, government documents, etc. His facts always check.

# QUERIED AGAIN.

One way to explain the work of the anthropologist is to tell the story of a series of conversations between Evarts and two members of Columbia University's department of anthropology—Dr. Alexander Lesser and his wife, Dr. Gene Weltfish. Evarts is a little past 75 now, but his body, except for failing eyes, is as sound as his memory, a memory from which he drew information which enabled Dr. Lesser to write a detailed, 337-paged anthropological monograph, "The Pawnee Ghost Dance Hand Game: A Study of Cultural Change."

When Dr. Lesser got through with him, Dr. Weltfish took over, questioning him over a period of weeks about the economic cycle of the Pawnee year and setting down a mass of notes which, when organized and typed, totaled more than 1,400 pages.

Evarts was an adolescent when the government moved the Pawnee from Nebraska south to Oklahoma, a trek which wrecked the tribe. (In 1838 the Pawnees were estimated at 12,000; there are about 600 left in the world.) His memory bridges the life of the tribe in both regions. Because he is intelligent and has an almost photogenic memory and because he has lived among white people and has had experiences which give him a basis of comparison Evarts is the kind of informant-interpreter anthropologists dream about.

The fact that he knew both white and Indian civilizations is important. The Indian who does not know a little about the ways of the white man is apt to think that the inquisitive anthropologist is a screwball.

## GETS SUSPICIOUS.

"When the investigator approaches a member of such a tribe (a tribe with no knowledge of white ways)," wrote Dr. Alexander Goldenweiser, another Columbia-trained anthropologist, in commenting on this matter, "his point of view is not at all apparent to the primitive."

"If the primitive understands the investigator at all, the fact that this strange fellow is puzzled by the obvious and is asking persistent questions about simple matters known to every child is not calculated to enhance the questioner's reputation for intelligence in the eyes of the informant. The latter, then, is likely to be suspicious of the anthropologist's motives and on his guard generally—a very unfavorable situation for successful field work."

Dr. Lesser and Dr. Weltfish did not have trouble of this kind with Evarts. After he had been prompted a little he began to unload his mind.

"He remembers situations," said Dr. Weltfish. "He has no interest in detail as such. His talk is a series of visual images, where he sat in the mud lodges, who sat across from him, what was on the altar, who danced and why, what they ate, and things like that. Once he listed 128 men by name who could have been invited to a certain feast, and then told me how many were invited. Then he told me why those who could have been invited were not. This was a feast that took place forty or fifty years ago."

## OFTEN CHECKED.

"We checked on his memory constantly and hardly ever found him wrong. For example, he worked at harness-making in Philadelphia for a period around 1893 for a Mr. Hanson, at 118 Market St., if you're interested. Well, he can sit out in Oklahoma and recall the squares of statues he saw in Philadelphia forty-four years ago. We went back and checked on the location of statues in Philadelphia of that date, and Evarts was always right."

"This is the way I worked with him. I would sit down and say:—'Suppose it was a day in spring. You are home from the winter hunt. You are sitting in the mud hut. Who is there with you? Where were the beds placed in the hut? How much corn did you take out of the pit that day and how much dried buffalo meat?' He would listen to my questions and then apparently a picture would come into his mind and he would start talking."

"He gave a beautifully detailed picture of Pawnee life. The Pawnee do not fit into the popular conception of the horse-riding, war-whooping, tepee-living Indian. From ancient times, as archaeologists have shown, these people were agricultural, raising the traditional Indian crops—corn, beans, squash."

"Their religious ideology was based on the cultivation of the earth. They lived in settled villages in well-made mud houses. They had a complex political organization of chiefs, a police system, a standing army, a priesthood. For part of the year they would go out in a body to hunt the buffalo. They had packhorses to bring the meat back. While they traveled the chiefs would determine which direction they should take, and the priests observed their rituals and the police kept order."

"I am telling you things sketchily that Evarts told in great detail. He described buffalo hunts, for example, with a wealth of detail, telling how many were killed one day and how many the next, who did the skinning, who did the packing. Sometimes they traveled long distances on a hunt. On one trip 2,000 persons went along and they traveled 150 miles. They had to take stores along, of course. That was a complex undertaking. Evarts made a map of one trip along the Platte River."

"Each summer for two months they hunted, and each winter for two months. After they hilled up their corn in the summer they would leave, returning with quantities of meat. After they had harvested the crops, storing them in cache-pits, and after they had fattened their horses, mended their clothes and put the skin tepees in order they would leave for the winter hunt. They ate well.

## FOOD IN CACHES.

"They kept their food in caches in the ground. The caches were bell shaped and sometimes seven feet deep. They were lined with grass and sticks and covered over with grass, wood-slats and earth. They tried not to open them when it snowed or rained because the moisture would rot the dried corn and squash and the jerked meats. Evarts told in detail how the houses were built, how long it took, who could give orders on construction jobs. I got from him a complete picture of an entire Pawnee year."

Dr. Weltfish and Dr. Lesser did a great deal of work on the Pawnee language with Evarts. Such work is exceedingly important to anthropologists, since a large number of American Indian languages are at the vanishing point. Many of those which are about to become extinct have been studied under the auspices of the Committee of Research in Native American Languages of the American Council of Learned

Societies. The preservation of these languages depend largely on such Indians as Evarts and Kai Kai, a wry old woman, the sole living person who still speaks the Southern Caddoan dialect, the language of a group of Indian tribes who once lived in southern Oklahoma, in Arkansas, and near the Red River in Louisiana. From the speech of this old woman, an Oklahoman, who belongs to the Kitsai tribe, Dr. Lesser has outlined the foundations of the language.

## VALUABLE PERSON.

Kai Kai has been about as valuable as Evarts, but she does not have his disposition. Aware that anthropologists consider her language the key to a considerable part of Amerind history, she knows her own value. Kai Kai is now almost 90. She pretends to be dull and sullen, but actually is an intelligent, energetic person. The last of her several husbands died more than forty years ago, and all her children and grandchildren are dead.

Since 1900 she has lived by herself—most of the time in a grass house. Several years ago she ordered the Indian agent at Anadarko, Oklahoma, to build her a two-room frame cottage and a backhouse. This he did. She leases all her government land allotment to white farmers, receiving a small amount of cash each week with which she carefully buys store groceries in Anadarko. She never travels farther than Anadarko which is eight miles from her home. In 1904 she visited the St. Louis Fair and the sight of the crowds filled her with disgust.

Most of the wrinkled, feeble men and women with whose help American anthropologists are reconstructing languages and tribal histories are obliged to dig painfully into their memories for detail of significance, and many consider their reminiscences of little value, preferring to speak of things as contemporary as the Townsend Plan. Evarts himself, for example, is a baseball and prize fight fan. He listens to sports broadcasts on the radio. He says he predicted the defeat of Joe Louis. He said, however, that he didn't bet against him.

"If I have money, he once explained, "I don't bet on fights. I buy beer."

—

*Tomorrow:—New Guinea business and social customs.*

—

*New York World-Telegram*
1937

# Man—With Variations

## People of Dobu Behave a Lot Like People on the Subway

*The sixth of a series.*

By JOSEPH MITCHELL
*World-Telegram Staff Writer*

There are people in many steam-heated, elaborately civilized societies who have things in common with the people who live in the tiny, scattered villages of the Dobu Islands, a group of scanty-soiled, volcanic upcroppings off the southern shore of eastern New Guinea. On those islands there are laws against thievery, but the thief is exalted if he can get away with it, people engage in endless business deals simply for the pleasure involved, cut-throat competition is the basis of all endeavor, and the people are always as dour and set-faced as the people in a subway.

Dr. R. F. Fortune lived for almost one year among the Dobu, gathering anthropological information. He landed on an island inhabited by forty persons, not one of whom knew more than two dozen words of English, and after his first day there he used no English at all, acquiring the language "by contagion." After three months with these forty people he found he knew the language so well that "nothing said passed over me, and nothing much in a quarrel with many shouting more or less simultaneously."

# TREACHERY VIRTUE.

Dr. Fortune found that the people of Dobu have a reputation for danger, constantly using magic and sorcery against one another. All the social forms put a premium upon ill-will and treachery and make them the recognized virtues of the society. A couple of generations ago they were cannibals. They have a hard time to grow enough yams in their carefully guarded patches to keep alive, and they are easy marks for labor recruiters. They sign up readily for indentured labor, and are favored work-boys because the coarse rations they receive do not cause them to mutiny. When a male Dobuan reaches puberty he is not permitted to sleep in his parents' home any longer, but is required to roam at night until he can find a bed in the room of a single girl. He must leave this room before daybreak. If he is caught after sunrise he is forced to marry the girl.

"Marriage is set in motion by a hostile act of the mother-in-law," stated Dr. Ruth Benedict, of the department of anthropology of Columbia University, who made a summary of Dr. Fortune's findings. "She blocks with her own person the door of the house within which the youth is sleeping with her daughter, and he is trapped for the public ceremony of betrothal.

## IT'S A GAME.

"Before this, since the time of puberty, the boy has slept each night in the houses of unmarried girls. By custom his own house is closed to him. He avoids entanglements for several years by spreading his favors and leaving the house well before daylight. When he is trapped at last it is usually because he has tired of his roaming and has settled on a more constant companion. He ceases to be so careful about early rising. Nevertheless he is never thought of as being ready to undertake the indignities of marriage, and the event is forced upon him by the old witch in the doorway, his future mother-in-law. When the villagers, the maternal kin of the girl, see the old woman immobile in her doorway they gather, and under the stare of the public the two descend and sit on a mat upon the ground. The villagers stare at them for half an hour and gradually disperse, nothing more; the couple are formally betrothed."

"From this time forward the young man has to reckon with the village of his wife. Its first demand is upon his labor. Immediately his mother-in-law gives him a digging stick with the command, "Now work." He must make a garden under the surveillance of his parents-in-law. When they cook and eat he must continue work, since he cannot eat in their presence.

## HEAVY BURDENS.

"He is bound to a double task, for when he has finished work on his father-in-law's yams he has still to cultivate his own garden on his own family land. His father-in-law gets ample satisfaction of his will to power and hugely enjoys his power over his son-in-law. For a year or more the situation continues. The boy is not the only one who is caught in this affair, for his relatives are loaded with obligations. So heavy are the burdens upon his brothers in providing the necessary garden stuff and the valuables for the marriage gift that nowadays young men at their brother's betrothal escape from the imposition by signing up with the white recruiter for indentured labor."

The material brought back by Dr. Fortune gives an exceedingly gloomy picture of a Dobu wedding party. There is no friendly mingling between the kin of the groom and the kin of the bride. A wide space separates them when they gather in the bride's village, and they appear unaware of each other's existence. If they do happen to notice the other party they glare with hostility. Before the marriage the bride's kin must go to the groom's village and sweep it throughout. They must also take a considerable gift of uncooked food. Next day the groom's kin appear with a reciprocal gift of yams.

## COOKERY EXCHANGE.

"The marriage itself," said Dr. Benedict, "consists in the groom's receiving from his mother-in-law in her village a mouthful of food of her cooking, and the bride's similarly receiving food from her mother-in-law in the village of her husband."

To make his anthropological study of the Dobu, a study which is known technically as an examination of "a test case of the working of bilocal residence under conditions of unilateral segmentation," Dr. Fortune lived in a hut which the natives built for him, ate the native food, fished with the natives, and went on trips with them. He broke up his stay by going to New Zealand for three months to recuperate.

"He did not find it necessary to 'go native' in Dobu," said Dr. Benedict. "It is not always wise for an anthropologist to do so. For one thing, government officials and white traders in such districts usually resent that approach. Before leaving Sydney, Australia, he got as many documents with gold seals on them as possible. Anthropologists seldom carry guns, and they have found that nothing impresses a colonial official so much as big gold seals. He talked with every official and missionary who could give him information about the Dobu before leaving for his study.

## DRESS CLOTHES.

"It might interest the general public to know that an anthropologist always takes dress clothes along if he is going to an English possession. He would lose prestige with the white officials if he turned up in rough and ready fashion, and he makes difficulties for himself if he does not get along well with the officials. We always advise women anthropologists to take along evening clothes, no matter how primitive the country to which she is going. Also, it is absolutely necessary for the anthropologists to arrive first-class when going to an English possession. There have been anthropologists who have worked on ships during several laps of their journey but who sailed first-class on the final lap."

"To work successfully the anthropologist must establish friendly relations with the natives. Each person has to do that in his own way, of course, but usually an anthropologist takes gifts along. Tobacco is the best gift. Anthropologists usually take along a supply of plug tobacco because it is compact. It can be shaved up for smoking."

"The belief that anthropologists always carry along quantities of five and ten cent store trinkets is erroneous. Sometimes a man will take along bundles of shiny trinkets and then find that the people he is to study have no interest at all in such things. His equipment usually consists of a typewriter, a camera and some simple medical supplies. Sometimes it is possible to establish friendly relations by distributing medicine, but in other cases that is the worst possible thing to do because it angers the native medicine men."

## NO BOREDOM.

"One might think that field workers get immensely bored living month after month among obscure primitives, but boredom is rare. The anthropologist is like a detective, and he must find his clues in the everyday, routine life around him. Usually he hates to leave a primitive society, feeling that things might turn up in one more week or one more month which could make his study far more valuable. In some societies, for example, there are rituals which take place every third year, and he might come the year before, missing something of great significance. Also, during his stay there might be no births and deaths. I am sure there have been times when anthropologists, hating to leave without obtaining authentic data on funeral rituals have yearned for a death in the tribe." ■

Also available from Prickly Paradigm Press:

*continued*

*continued*